GENETIC ENGINEERING
AND Developments in Biotechnology

Crabtree Publishing Company
www.crabtreebooks.com

Anne Rooney

Crabtree Publishing Company

www.crabtreebooks.com

Author: Anne Rooney

Series research and development: Reagan Miller

Editorial director: Kathy Middleton

Photo research: James Nixon

Editors: Paul Humphrey, James Nixon, and Philip Gebhardt

Proofreader: Wendy Scavuzzo

Layout: sprout.uk.com

Cover design and logo: Margaret Amy Salter

Production coordinator and prepress technician: Margaret Amy Salter

Print coordinator: Katherine Berti

Consultant: Carolyn de Cristofano, M.Ed. STEM consultant, Professional Development Director of Engineering is Elementary (2005–2008)

Production coordinated by Discovery Books

Photographs:
Alamy: pp. 5 (imageBROKER), 12 (Prisma Bildagentur AG), 13 bottom (BSIP SA), 14 (Deco), 15 top (BSIP SA), 15 bottom (Sergio Azenha), 16 (BSIP SA), 22 top (Aurora Photos), 24 bottom (Irene Abdou), 26 (Nature Picture Library).
Bigstock: pp. 6 (monkeybusiness-images), 7 bottom (designua), 8 right (Kovalevska), 9 middle (Jagodka), 17 top (Awakened), 17 bottom (monkeybusiness-images), 18 top (Odua Images), 18 bottom (tilo), 19 (Brian Lasenby), 21 top (mshhoward), 21 bottom (Aleksandr Nekhayev), 22 bottom (Eraxion), 24 top (Kletr), 25 (Paha_L), 28 (searagen), 29 bottom (Elenarts).
Getty Images: pp. 13 top (Steve Jennings/Stringer), 20 (Li Xiang/Xinhua Press/Corbis), 23 (Michael Smith).
Wikimedia: pp. 4 (International Rice Research Institute), 7 top (Maggie Bartlett/NHGRI), 8 left and middle (John Doebley), 9 top and bottom, 10 top, 10 bottom (Cudmore), 11 top and bottom (Smithsonian Institution Archives), 27 (www.glofish.com), 29 top (NASA).

All other images by Shutterstock

Library and Archives Canada Cataloguing in Publication

Rooney, Anne, author
    Genetic engineering and developments in biotechnology / Anne Rooney.

(Engineering in action)
Includes index.
Issued in print and electronic formats.
ISBN 978-0-7787-7538-6 (hardback).--
ISBN 978-0-7787-7542-3 (paperback).--
ISBN 978-1-4271-1787-8 (html)

        1. Genetic engineering--Juvenile literature. 2. Biotechnology--Juvenile literature. I. Title. II. Series: Engineering in action (St. Catharines, Ont.)

QH442.R66 2016   j660.6'5   C2016-903295-7
                                       C2016-903296-5

Library of Congress Cataloging-in-Publication Data

Names: Rooney, Anne, author.
Title: Genetic engineering and developments in biotechnology / Anne Rooney.
Description: St. Catharines, Ontario ; New York, NY : Crabtree Publishing Company, [2016] | Series: Engineering in action | Includes index.
Identifiers: LCCN 2016027297 (print) | LCCN 2016028629 (ebook) | ISBN 9780778775386 (reinforced library binding : alk. paper) | ISBN 9780778775423 (pbk. : alk. paper) | ISBN 9781427117878 (Electronic HTML)
Subjects: LCSH: Biotechnology--Juvenile literature. | Genetic engineering--Juvenile literature. | Technological innovations--Juvenile literature.
Classification: LCC QH442 .R66 2016 (print) | LCC QH442 (ebook) | DDC 660.6--dc23
LC record available at https://lccn.loc.gov/2016027297

Crabtree Publishing Company
www.crabtreebooks.com   1-800-387-7650

Printed in Canada/072016/EF20160630

Published in Canada
Crabtree Publishing
616 Welland Ave.
St. Catharines, ON
L2M 5V6

Published in the United States
Crabtree Publishing
PMB 59051
350 Fifth Avenue, 59th Floor
New York, New York 10118

Published in the United Kingdom
Crabtree Publishing
Maritime House
Basin Road North, Hove
BN41 1WR

Published in Australia
Crabtree Publishing
3 Charles Street
Coburg North
VIC, 3058

CONTENTS

WHAT IS GENETIC ENGINEERING?

Glow-in-the-dark kittens, foods with extra **nutrients**, and bananas that contain vaccines, are the types of things designed and produced by genetic engineers. These engineers work with a wide range of plants, animals, and **microorganisms**. They add or improve desirable characteristics, and remove or reduce unwanted characteristics, by changing what goes on inside the organism's **cells**. Genetic engineering has immense potential. It holds the promise of feeding the world, curing disease, and fixing pollution.

Engineering and science: Engineers often work with the information discovered by scientists, putting it to practical use to design things that people want. Scientists work to find out how **genes** affect the way organisms, including humans, grow and work. Genetic engineers then use this information to change organisms, so they grow and function in ways we want them to. For example, medical scientists discovered a chemical associated with development of the disease Alzheimer's, which leads to damage in the brain. Genetic engineers worked out which gene leads to production of the chemical, then put it into a transparent worm. By studying the way the disease develops in worms, medical scientists hope to understand better how it develops in humans.

"Golden rice" is genetically engineered rice that helps to provide vitamin A to people in areas where their diets are poor. The rice is yellow, while ordinary rice is white.

EIGHT STEPS TO SUCCESS

Genetic engineers follow an eight-step process to develop their projects (right). It covers designing, implementing, testing, and improving solutions. In other types of engineering, engineers design a **prototype** of their solution. But in genetic engineering they implement part of the project and test it.

Engineers at work

Genetic engineers can work in any of these fields:

- Agriculture (farming): changing the characteristics of crops (plants) or animals so they produce more food and are easier to keep or grow

- Medicine: working to fix or prevent diseases that are inherited (passed down through families), and using microorganisms such as **bacteria** to produce medicines

- Environmental management: changing crops to reduce the need for pesticides (chemicals that kill insect pests)

- Research: developing new techniques to use in genetic engineering

- Conservation: working to save endangered animals, and even bring back **extinct** organisms

Some areas of genetic engineering raise issues people disagree about, particularly those that involve working with humans and animals. Many people are excited by the prospects offered by genetic engineering. But some object to what genetic engineers might do, either on purpose or by accident.

Steps in the development process

Define the problem

↓

Identify criteria and constraints

↓

Brainstorm ideas

↓

Select a solution

↓

Implement the project

↓

Test the project

↓

Modify the project

↓

Share the solution

Genetic engineering involves precise work in the laboratory.

HOW GENES WORK

All organisms inherit characteristics from their parents. You can probably see that you share some features with your parents and any brothers or sisters you have. These characteristics are carried in genes—chemical codes carried in most cells in the body.

Every gene holds a recipe for a single **protein** that the organism can produce. Together, these proteins produce the organism's characteristics and control how it works. For example, there are proteins that make a hair black and proteins that help you digest food. If a protein is changed, or not made, that will produce a change in the organism. It can be a good change, a bad change, or a change that doesn't make much difference—an eye works just as well if it is blue or brown, for instance. When genetic engineers make changes to organisms, they change the proteins that are being made by the organism.

Passing it on

Many plants and animals reproduce sexually, meaning they have two parents. Half of the new organism's genes come from each parent, mixing characteristics from each. Microorganisms such as bacteria reproduce asexually—there is only one parent. Ordinarily, each new organism is an exact copy of the parent, with all the same genes.

Members of a family share genetic similarities, but there are differences between individuals.

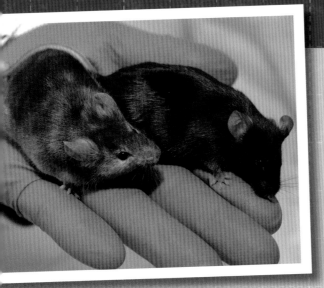

Genetic engineers can add, remove, or change genes to alter how an organism looks, behaves, or functions. To know which genes to change, it is necessary to work out what each gene does. They do this by "knocking out" (removing) genes from a developing organism, and seeing which feature is affected. They can do this with microorganisms, plants, and laboratory animals such as mice.

The mouse on the left has had a gene relating to hair growth knocked out and has less fur.

Genes, chromosomes, DNA: Each gene is a specific area of a long strand of a complex chemical called DNA. The strand is called a chromosome. Chromosomes are the genetic material of the organism and carry all the information needed for the organism to grow and function. There are complete copies of all the chromosomes in nearly every cell of the body.

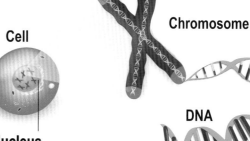

Cell

Chromosome

Nucleus (contains important parts of the cell, including DNA)

DNA

Gene

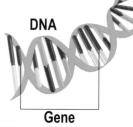

Genes are strung together in a sequence on chromosomes.

THE HUMAN GENOME PROJECT

Humans have 46 chromosomes. The Human **Genome** Project aimed to discover and list all the genes on these chromosomes. (The entire collection of an organism's gene is called its genome.) The project was officially completed in 2003. Simply listing more than 20,000 human genes is very different from knowing each gene's function. Scientists are still working to find out what each gene does.

BIGGER, BETTER, WOOLLIER

Humans have been changing animals and plants for thousands of years. In the past, this was through the slow process of selective breeding—choosing animals or plants with desirable characteristics and breeding them.

Early farmers made farming more productive through selective breeding. They chose the woolliest sheep or the cows that produced the most milk, and bred them. The result was more sheep with thick wool or cows that gave a lot of milk. They kept seeds from the corn or wheat that produced the best grains, and planted that the following year. Over several generations, the features that people wanted in plants and animals were reinforced.

Modern corn (right) has been produced by selective breeding from a natural form with fewer, smaller grains (left.)

ROBERT BAKEWELL

Robert Bakewell (1725-1795) was a British farmer with an interest in improving farming. He kept male and female animals apart, only bringing together individuals of his choosing to breed. By doing this, the offspring were more likely to inherit particular characteristics. This method of breeding allowed Bakewell to produce new breeds of sheep, cattle that grew meat more quickly, and strong sturdy horses.

Pekingese dogs have been bred to have broad, flat faces. The dogs commonly have breathing difficulties as a result.

Genes are at work in selective breeding, but people don't need to understand what is going on inside the organisms to make it work. Our ancestors discovered that they could improve their herds and crops in this way. Selective breeding has produced better farm animals and food crops, faster horses, stronger oxen for pulling carts or machinery, and more attractive features in pets. It's still used today. It is cheaper than genetic engineering and does not require complex technology.

Selective breeding only works with animals or plants that can breed together. Genetic engineering is more flexible and more precise. It can work with specific individual genes, and can also combine genes from different species that could not **interbreed**. For example, genetically modified (GM) blue roses have been made by adding a gene from pansies. Roses and pansies could never combine naturally.

This rose, named "Applause," is a product of genetic engineering.

TOWARD GENETIC ENGINEERING

While selective breeding can be done without genetic knowledge or special equipment, genetic engineering only became possible when people understood how genes work, then developed sophisticated techniques and tools.

From peas to flies

Progress began in the 1860s when the Czech scientist Gregor Mendel carried out many controlled experiments with pea plants, which he **crossed** with one another. He discovered that characteristics are inherited following a mathematical pattern, but he didn't know how the biological process worked.

In 1883, the Belgian biologist Edouard van Beneden discovered chromosomes in cell nuclei. The idea that chromosomes might be responsible for inherited characteristics was suggested in 1903. The following year, Thomas Hunt Morgan opened the "Fly Room," a laboratory in Columbia University, New York, where he worked breeding fruit flies. He proved that chromosomes carry the inherited characteristics, and produced the first-ever gene map showing where genes are on a chromosome.

Thomas Hunt Morgan's work with fruit flies became the foundation of modern genetic engineering.

Fruit flies are very tiny insects, often kept in flasks by scientists. They reproduce quickly and easily, making them useful for experiments in genetics.

First tools: For many years, the technology did not exist for scientists and engineers to use their knowledge. Chromosomes are long, complex **molecules** and people did not know how to break them apart or move parts around. Then, in 1973, the American scientist Paul Berg became the first to combine DNA from different organisms, now called recombinant DNA. He worked with two different **viruses**. Both have DNA that forms a closed loop. He used an **enzyme** to "cut" open each loop, then added another enzyme to make the ends stick together into a single large loop.

The method of cutting open DNA and adding a new section became the standard technique. It became known as "gene splicing." Chemicals are used for all operations with genes because genes are too small to be manipulated with physical tools.

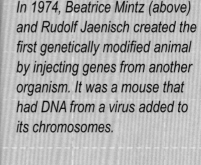

In 1974, Beatrice Mintz (above) and Rudolf Jaenisch created the first genetically modified animal by injecting genes from another organism. It was a mouse that had DNA from a virus added to its chromosomes.

Barbara McClintock, 1947

BARBARA McCLINTOCK AND "JUMPING GENES"

Barbara McClintock was an American geneticist who worked with corn plants. One of her most important pieces of work was proving that genes do not have to occupy a fixed place on a chromosome. When she made her discovery in the 1930s, it was dismissed. But the idea was later accepted, and she won the Nobel Prize for Physiology in 1983.

HOW GENETIC ENGINEERING WORKS

Genetic engineers can add entire genes to an organism's genome. They can also remove entire genes. When necessary, they can make changes to individual genes in the genome.

Adding and taking away

Each protein the body uses is produced by the action of a gene, so removing (knocking out) a gene stops an organism making one of its proteins. Many inherited diseases are the result of the body failing to make a particular protein because a gene is missing. Animals that have genes knocked out are often bred to test medicines. In 2015, genetic engineers in China removed a gene that limits muscle growth from the **embryo** of a dog. The dog that was born kept growing muscles. Producing dogs with this defect will be of help in investigating muscle diseases.

Adding a gene can introduce a specific trait to an organism. A gene from a fish called an ocean pout added to a salmon genetically modifies the salmon and makes it grow faster.

People with **diabetes** often can't produce insulin—a protein used by the body to process sugar. For these people, daily insulin therapy is an important part of diabetes treatment. An adequate supply of insulin must be produced to meet their needs. Since the 1980s, insulin for treating diabetes has been made by bacteria that have had an insulin-producing gene added.

Insulin and other products made by genetically engineered microorganisms are produced in large vats in which bacteria are grown.

New tools: Traditional gene splicing is an expensive and slow process. Genetic engineers have to design a new chemical each time to lock onto the right gene and cut it out of the DNA.

A new technique called CRISPR is much cheaper and easier to employ. Developed by American biologist Jennifer Doudna and French geneticist Emmanuelle Charpentier, it was first used in

Jennifer Doudna (left) and Emmanuelle Charpentier (right) at the Breakthrough Prize Awards Ceremony.

2013. CRISPR uses a harmless virus to carry three components into the cell nucleus: a "guide molecule," a protein called Cas9, and the new chunk of DNA. Cas9 cuts the DNA where the guide molecule indicates, and the new chunk of DNA fits into the gap. CRISPR can be used in a single-cell embryo, changing the chromosomes from which all others will be copied as the organism grows. It can also be used to edit genes in particular cells in an adult organism. In this way, CRISPR might be used to damage the DNA of cancer cells to prevent the growth of the cancer.

Research in a genetics lab is carried out under **sterile** conditions—any contamination can destroy the work.

CLONES

Cloning produces a genetically identical copy of an organism. Genetic engineers first remove the DNA from an egg cell of the appropriate animal. They then take DNA from the organism being copied and put it into the egg cell. The egg then grows into a copy of the original organism. It's very useful because it produces identical genetically modified organisms. Many copies of an organism might be needed for medical research, for example.

WORKING IN GENETIC ENGINEERING

Most genetic engineers work in laboratories connected to commercial organizations, universities, hospitals, or research institutes. Some genetic engineers work with human genes (on medical projects), with animals, or with plants, but many work with microorganisms. Often, a project involves more than one type of organism.

Jobs in genetic engineering involve precise laboratory work with specialized, expensive, and fragile equipment, as well as chemicals. The work requires accuracy and attention to detail. To work in this field, you will need a good general and scientific education. You will need to be able to work in a specialized, sterile environment, and observe strict working practices to ensure safety and reliability.

Genetic engineers work with tiny samples and small quantities of chemicals.

CAREER SPOTLIGHT

Rasha is a 24-year-old **postgraduate** student. Her first degree was in biotechnology. Now Rasha works on genetic-engineering approaches to disease. Her work currently involves raising piglets that have been genetically modified to have a muscle disease that also affects humans. She uses the piglets to test a new treatment for the human disease. She supervises the care of the piglets, and spends time administering treatments and taking samples from the animals. She checks the samples in the laboratory to find out if the genetic changes have been successful, and to see if the treatment is working.

Plants used in genetic engineering must be carefully looked after to ensure that the work is successful.

Many jobs require at least a degree, and usually a postgraduate degree. But there are also roles for lab technicians and assistants, and jobs tending plants or animals used in **trials** and projects.

Skills: Genetic engineering projects are large, expensive, long-term endeavors that combine the expertise and dedication of many people, so you will need to be able to work in a team. Creativity and an ability to think logically will enable you to see unusual solutions to problems, and think through methods and possible outcomes. You will need good communication skills, too, since you will need to present your ideas to colleagues and possibly the public.

A large genetics laboratory often has many people working in it, each performing a different role.

BEFORE STARTING

The design process is not quite the same in genetic engineering as in other types of engineering because genetic engineers work with living organisms. In addition, there are **ethical** and safety concerns that sometimes extend beyond the individual project.

Working ethically: Any work with humans or laboratory animals must meet strict ethical and safety rules. That means genetic engineers must not cause unnecessary harm or suffering, or take unacceptable risks.

Other ethical questions are hotly debated: people disagree about what is acceptable. Some people object to any interference with genes because they consider it wrong. Some object to research or techniques that use cells from human embryos. Some people think it is wrong to mix genes from different species.

TRADE-OFFS

There are trade-offs to consider in any project and these can include ethical trade-offs. For example, medicines are often tested on animals specially bred to have the disease the medicine aims to treat. There is a trade-off between the suffering of the animals and the potential benefits to humans.

When working with animals, genetic engineers need to follow rules about how they treat them.

Working safely: Genetic engineering is relatively new. We have not had time to discover any unintended consequences. Some people worry that genetically modified organisms might spread their genes through wild populations and other species, causing harm. Some people believe that we all have a right to know what we are eating and what is around us. If someone is allergic to fish for example, might they respond badly to a vegetable with a fish gene in it?

Protestors object to genetically modified organisms (GMOs).

Changes before birth

As genetic engineering offers more approaches to treating disease, there are some tricky choices to make. Some genetic diseases could be prevented entirely by changing the genes in a single-celled embryo. This would affect all future generations from that embryo. Is it right or safe to make changes to humans that will be passed on forever, even if they are beneficial changes?

The benefits genetic engineering might bring to human health in the form of treatments must be weighed against the harm caused to any animals.

WE HAVE A PROBLEM...

The design process begins with identifying a problem, specifying the criteria the solution must meet, and considering the constraints that will limit what can be done. The next stage in tackling a problem is brainstorming—coming up with as many approaches as possible. Ideas are critically examined later.

Feeding babies

Some mothers can't or don't want to feed their babies with their own milk, and therefore give them artificial baby milk (formula) instead. But formula does not contain all the nutrients of human milk. There are different ways of approaching the problem of nutrition for these babies. We could make better formula, or look for a new solution. Human milk is a very complex mix of chemicals, and traditional methods of copying it by adding chemicals to cow milk have gone as far as they can for now. A genetic engineering solution is to modify another animal to produce milk that mimics human milk. The criteria are that the milk must be better for babies than existing formula, as well as easy and inexpensive to produce on a large scale.

A better match to human milk, produced by genetically engineered cows, would benefit bottle-fed babies.

Cows are a good choice for producing human-like milk because dairy-farming of cattle is already well established.

Constraints: In any engineering project, there are constraints that limit what can be done. These often include cost, safety, and ethical concerns. Any substitute for human milk must be safe to drink, for example. If cows that produce human-like milk are very expensive or difficult to keep, the solution won't work economically. Ethical concerns include deciding whether cows would suffer from the process, and whether it is wrong to put human genes into a cow.

BRAINSTORMING AND BEES

In Canada, honeybees are dying from disease. The reduced number of bees affects crop **pollination** and honey production. There are several possible approaches to this problem:
· Seek a cure for diseases that kill bees
· Import bees to replace the lost hives
· Produce genetically engineered bees that are resistant to disease

Many honeybees die in the cold, so introducing new strains is not easy. The genetic engineering solution looks promising. A project at the University of British Columbia plans to find 12 characteristics of honeybees that can be combined in genetically engineered bees resistant to both cold and disease.

Genetically modified bees could solve the problem of bee deaths in Canada and elsewhere.

MAKING CHOICES

After brainstorming, genetic engineers choose the most promising idea and begin to implement the approach. The choice will depend on many factors, taking into account the criteria and constraints of the project, as well as the trade-offs that need to be made.

Choosing an approach: A project overseen by Professor Ning Li at China Agricultural University in Beijing took a genetic-engineering approach to making better baby milk. The team had to choose which animal to use to produce the milk, and which changes to make to its genes. They chose to use cows. A similar project in California chose to use goats. There might be two or more equally valid approaches, but the genetic-engineering team chooses the approach that best fits their aims, experience, and resources.

Ning's team looked at ingredients that are in human milk but not in cow's milk. They chose three proteins that help the baby's immune system (the system that protects the baby from disease). Genetic engineers and scientists identified the human genes that are responsible for these chemicals in human milk, and decided to put the genes into Holstein dairy cows.

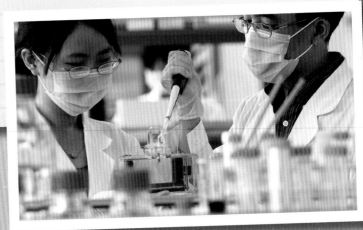

China is leading many of the advances in genetic engineering.

PEST-PROOF

Traditionally, farmers have used chemical pesticides to protect crops from insects. Genetic engineering offers a new solution that is more friendly to the environment. Corn, cotton, and soybeans can all have a gene added that makes them produce their own pesticide chemicals.

A field of genetically engineered cotton requires less crop spraying than natural cotton.

Mammoths died out in Siberia 10,000 years ago. Could genetic engineering bring them back to life?

BACK FROM THE DEAD?

Sergey Zimov, director of the Northeast Science Station in Cherkii, Russia, wants to recreate ice-age animals and release them into the frozen wastelands of Siberia. Two possible approaches are being investigated. George Church at Harvard Medical School hopes to combine elephant and mammoth DNA to create a near-mammoth. A Russian-Korean team wants to put mammoth DNA into an elephant egg cell and produce a complete mammoth. There are interesting ethical questions here. Do we have the right to bring back extinct creatures that will have an effect on the animals that currently live in that environment? And who gets to choose whether we do it?

DOES IT WORK?

Once genetic engineers have implemented a technique, they run tests to see how well it works. First trials are often on single cells. They test whether the DNA has been correctly modified, for example. If the work is with animals, the next stage might involve test animals of a species that is easy to work with. Mice are often used since they mature and reproduce quickly, so genetic engineers can work with many generations in a short period. The final stage involves growing the organism they have designed, and testing its function. Does it do what is required? Is it healthy?

Mice are often used in genetic research. They are genetically similar to humans, and it is relatively easy to make genetic changes to them.

From mice to cows

On Ning's milk project, the team worked with mice for many years, adding the chosen human genes to their genome and testing the results. Once the technique had been perfected with mice, the genetic engineers repeated it with cows. They produced a herd of 300 dairy cattle that could make milk that is 80 percent identical to human milk. They did this by adding human genes to DNA taken from the cow, then placing a modified egg cell into a cow to grow into a calf.

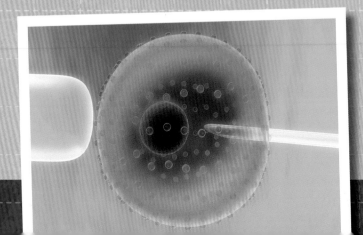

Work with a single egg cell is carried out looking through a microscope.

Once the calves grew up and were old enough to produce milk, the milk was first tested chemically to make sure it contained the proteins the genetic engineers expected. It was fed first to baby pigs to check that it was safe. It will be tested on adult humans before being given to babies. It's important to check there are no unintended side effects of the altered genes.

Refining the process: Although the cows made milk to the desired specification, there was a low success rate producing the animals themselves. Cloned animals of many types often die before, at, or soon after birth. Large-scale commercial production of cows that produce human milk will have to wait for refinements in cloning techniques to be developed. Other improvements the team might make to their project in the future include altering more genes so they add more human proteins to the milk, making it a better match for human milk.

The world's first cloned piglets were born in 2000 in the United States. They are all genetically identical.

SHARING RESULTS

Genetic engineers and scientists share their results by publishing papers in **journals**, giving talks at conferences, and writing books. Sharing the solution is an important step in the design process. If the project is successful, there is often a product to share or sell, too. It is even valuable to share the results of projects that fail or have limitations. It helps other people avoid the same mistakes, so the entire field can progress.

An Anopheles mosquito, red from its meal of blood.

Nearly there?

Malaria is a deadly tropical disease caused by a **parasite**. Forty percent of the world's population lives in areas affected by malaria and the disease killed an estimated 438,000 people in 2015. The parasite is transmitted from person to person by female Anopheles mosquitoes.

There have been several attempts at using genetic engineering to tackle malaria. One approach is to make mosquitoes produce only male offspring (which would wipe them out in a short time). Others are to make the mosquitoes incapable of feeding on humans, or of carrying the malaria parasite. An approach developed in 2015 involves releasing male mosquitoes genetically adapted so that the eggs they fertilize will never develop into adults. The latest trials also use a technique called "gene drive," which makes the desired gene more likely to be passed on when animals breed.

Two children in Africa sleep inside a mosquito net to protect themselves against malaria-carrying mosquitoes.

As every team publishes results of its trials, with successes and failures, the whole community moves closer to solving the problem of malaria. It also keeps debate active concerning ethical and safety issues. Is it right or safe to wipe out an entire species just to benefit humans? Other animals eat mosquitoes and their larvae—could wiping out these mosquitoes have unwanted effects on the ecosystem?

New techniques: Some genetic engineers are engaged in solving particular problems, such as how to engineer flood-tolerant crops, or make bacteria that will "eat" pollution. Others are engaged in developing tools and techniques that can be used in many projects. Recent successes have been the CRISPR method of gene-editing and the gene-drive method of forcing a gene to spread quickly through a population. Sharing these tools drives progress in all areas of genetic engineering.

Professionals can share results and lessons at conferences even before their work is published.

DESIGN CHALLENGE

You can't actually try genetic engineering yourself, but you can think about some of the issues involved and plan a project that a team of genetic engineers could carry out.

1. Define a problem you want to address: It could be to produce lettuce that won't be eaten by caterpillars, for example, or to produce a fruit that includes a nutrient not usually found in it. You might design a modification to a farm animal or crop that would make it more profitable to farm, or easier to store and transport to stores.

2. Specify the criteria for the design, and any constraints: If you are working with an animal or plant, are there conditions it needs to survive? Could you market your product? It will need to be inexpensive enough to produce so that people will be able to afford it.

3. Brainstorm the problem: Think of as many ways as possible to address the problem. Don't pause to criticize your ideas. You can do that later.

Genetic engineers can take the glow-in-the-dark gene from organisms such as this fungus to make other organisms glow.

4. Which solution would you select from your brainstorming session? Which genetic engineering techniques could you use? Will you be adding or removing genes, for instance? Will you need to clone organisms?

5. List and discuss the arguments for and against the modification you have designed: These should include practical, safety, and ethical issues. If you thought of making animals easier to handle in some way, would this affect their ability to look after themselves? Would the adjustment cause the animal distress or make its life worse? If your project would harm animals in any way, can you justify the trade-off, or should you change or abandon your project?

6. How would you test your solution? Think about how you would check that changes have been made to the genes, and whether the changes do what you had hoped they would do.

7. Make any adjustments to improve your plan regarding the practical and ethical issues you have considered.

8. If you shared your solution, could it be extended by other engineers to other types of animals or crops? If it is a medical project, could it have other applications?

Glowing fish are genetically modified fish sold as pets.

INTO THE FUTURE

Genetic engineering offers hope for the future in many areas. The ability to make crops that can withstand harsh conditions, produce improved **yield**, and include extra nutrients could help us to feed the growing world population.

TREES THAT CLEAN

Genetically modified microorganisms or plants could even help us to clean up the environment by breaking down **pollutants**. Sharon Doty at the University of Washington has developed poplar trees that can clean 91 percent of a common pollutant, trichloroethylene, from water in the ground.

Trees could be an inexpensive, environmentally friendly way to clean groundwater.

A cure for all?

A new technique uses harmless viruses to carry bits of DNA into the human body. In the future, this could be used as a way to cure genetic diseases. A virus could carry a corrected gene into someone's body to replace faulty genes that cause an illness. We might even be able to eliminate some genetic diseases by preventing their passage from parents to babies. However, that raises its own ethical questions. Who would choose which diseases should be wiped out? Are some inherited conditions just differences rather than illnesses?

We might be able to use crops to produce human chemicals that are needed as medicines. A research team in China is attempting to develop a strain of rice that produces proteins found in human blood. People with certain blood disorders could be treated simply by eating the special rice.

BUGS IN SPACE

NASA has engineered a type of bacteria that can produce plastics! The bacteria can be taken into space where they will make large quantities of plastic. Astronauts could then use it to make equipment. Carrying equipment into space is costly because it increases the weight of the spacecraft. Taking just a few bacteria into space, then letting them reproduce and make plastics, would be an inexpensive, simple solution.

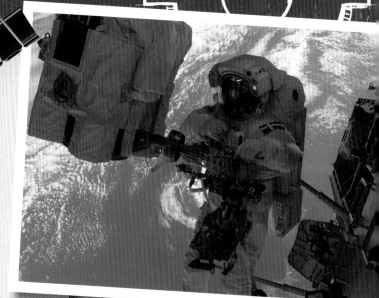

Astronauts might be able to make components and tools they need from plastic grown in space.

Using the CRISPR gene-editing method, it's becoming much easier and less expensive to alter organisms. This raises difficult questions for the future about what it is right or safe. How would you feel about people designing and creating unusual animals to keep as pets? What if you could have a tiny dinosaur as a pet? Is it wise or even safe to release modified organisms into the wild?

It's impossible to bring dinosaurs back from extinction, but we might one day be able to create dinosaur-like animals. Would it be right to do so?

LEARNING MORE

BOOKS

Barber, Nicola. *Both Sides of the Story: Cloning and Genetic Engineering*. Franklin Watts, 2014.

Gray, Leon. *Genetic Modification: Should Humans Control Nature?* Franklin Watts, 2015.

Merino, Noël (editor). *Genetic Engineering* (Opposing Viewpoints). Greenhaven Press, 2013.

Thompson, Tamara. *Genetically Modified Food* (At Issue). Greenhaven Press, 2014.

ONLINE

http://learn.genetics.utah.edu
A guide to genetics and its uses in human health.

www.yourgenome.org
An introduction to genetics and genetic engineering including its impact on society, from the Wellcome Genome Campus.

http://agbiosafety.unl.edu/basic_genetics.shtml
An explanation of genetic engineering techniques, University of Nebraska, Lincoln.

www.youtube.com/watch?v=_IgSDVD4QEc
Cracking the Code of Life. *The history of the Human Genome Project.*

PLACES TO VISIT

DNA Learning Center
Cold Spring Harbor, NY
www.dnalc.org
The world's largest genetics study lab is open to to the public at certain times of the year.

Mendel Museum of Genetics
Masaryk University
Czech Republic
http://mendelmuseum.muni.cz/en
A museum devoted to Gregor Mendel, known as the father of genetics.

GLOSSARY

bacteria Single-celled microorganisms that reproduce quickly

cell The smallest living component of an animal or plant body; all bodies are made up cells of different types (e.g., skin cells, bone cells)

chromosome A long strand of the chemical compound DNA on which sequences of chemicals form a code, which is divided into genes

crossed Put together to produce offspring

diabetes A serious disease in which a person's body cannot control the amount of sugar in its blood

DNA Short for deoxyribonucleic acid; a complex chemical with a structure formed of two strands twisted together like a twisted ladder

embryo A group of cells that will develop into an organism ready to be born or to hatch

enzyme A chemical which increases the rate of a chemical reaction, but is not used up in the process

ethical Relating to the moral status of an action or process

extinct Has completely died out

gene A segment of a chromosome that carries the coded instructions for making a single protein used by an organism

genome An organism's complete set of genes

interbreed To cause animals to produce young animals which are a mixture of two species

journal A magazine in which professionals who are focused on a particular field share information and the results of their work

microorganism An organism too small to see without a microscope

molecule The smallest component of a substance

nucleus (plural nuclei) The most important part of a cell that has a nucleus (some don't); it contains crucial structures and most of the DNA of the cell

nutrient A substance that humans, animals, and plants need to live and grow

parasite An organism that lives on or in another, benefitting from the other organism but not providing any benefit to it

pollination A process by which reproduction happens in plants, producing a seed from which a new plant can grow

pollutant A chemical which causes pollution in the environment (e.g. in the air, soil, or water)

postgraduate Relating to studies done after completing a university degree

protein An important class of chemicals essential to life; proteins are the structural building blocks of all organisms, and also perform important functions as enzymes and antibodies (chemicals that help the body fight disease)

prototype An early model of a design built to test the design's function

sterile Completely clean and free from contamination by germs

trials Tests of the quality, value, or usefulness of something

virus A very simple organism that can cause an infectious disease

yield The amount of produce generated by crops or farm animals

INDEX